THE STARE

HIDDEN
Included

S. E. McKenzie

DEDICATION
To everyone who has been left out in the cold

TABLE OF CONTENTS

THE STARE

THE STARE
I

You knew it wasn't fair
Wherever you went
They had to stare.

As if you weren't really there.

The Stare was everywhere;
The glare of hate and the toxic state
Was the pull of Monopolistic Power

To make it his own
He excluded others all around
Even those who shared his ground;

How did legislating poverty oppress?

Victim of process
Had no access
Or no address

And Monopolistic Man; a shell of a man;
Didn't care;
He traded his water and air

THE STARE: Hidden Included

For cold cash which just got devalued.

His snobocracy
Was the new aristocracy
Hidden behind words of an old meritocracy.

His Monopolistic Style flared his stare
While his rage grew
Between his eyes.

His glare needed no disguise
It pierced through your personal space,
His stare surrounded your face

As if you weren't there.

Marginalized and excluded;
Many said they cared
About their water and air

Beware of the Fallen Angel

Under his spell of hypocrisy
His self-fulfilling prophecy
Can come true

How did legislating poverty oppress?

Victim of process
Had no access
Or no address.

Under reconstruction
With barriers and obstruction
Never questioned the lies and his corruption

For this man so monopolistic
Was naturally simplistic
At times even sadistic

As he traded the water and air
For cold cash
Which just got devalued.

He demanded
Monopolistic Control
Without disguise

Even though
A Pluralistic Goal
Was far more a Natural Role.

THE STARE: Hidden Included

There was no compromise

For Internal Controls
Change on demand
Not on command;

External Controls
Guns and bombs
No faith in love;

As monopolistic man's rage grew
He demanded one way control
Never remembering a name

Because as he stared
Everyone looked the same
In his very own sum-zero game

There was always someone to blame
For the winner; life would never be the same
As Monopolistic Man grew into the dominant role.

His child dreamed
His wife screamed
For Monopolistic Man had his foot in the door

He said, "this is the only social order that is right
One way; one fight
My way every night

Or take the only highway in sight.
If you won't show deference to me
It is your loss, I am the boss

I don't want you here no more;

I will close every single door;
Surrounding you
Never to open the way doors did before."

And Monopolistic Man said,
"There is no goal greater than mine
For my One-Way-World suits me fine."

And they all held on to the key
Their way to fight
Against their own poverty.

The power to share was the multiplier
Though Monopolistic Man; a shell of a man;
Called Truth a liar

THE STARE: Hidden Included

Love watched as many died.
Love was ignored but could still inspire
As the solution was burning in Truth's fire

Love had a pulse and a heart
Love watched the overkill
Of the underfed and cried

Monopolistic Man
Journeys through life
Possessing what he can

Monopolistic Man; a shell of a man;
Becomes a killing machine
When needing a way to fulfill his dream

While his child dreamed
His wife screamed
Monopolistic Man had his foot in the door

Hell's Hate closed the gate
During this monopolistic fate
More than just another State of Hate.

Affordable pads were called slums
The tenants were all called bums
Love was an equalizer; you know it was true,

But Monopolistic Man; a shell of a man;
Needed a slave
Just like you.

How could you know
What your future had in store
When Monopolistic Man demanded so much more?

There was a path
That you were not allowed on
For it was behind the gate which controlled fate.

To take the path was the goal of some.
While Monopolistic Man; a shell of a man;
Called this act trespass against his class.

For the gate to equal opportunity
Was closed; buried under clause after clause
And Monopolistic Man said,

THE STARE: Hidden Included

"Follow the One-Way-Rule
For going the wrong way
Makes you a fool."

Monopolistic Man ruled by his might.
Every wrong; he called right;
He threw us fire when he promised light;

Self-fulfilling prophecy
Needed no light to see
For his Way was the only way

For Pluralistic Goals just got in the way
And they were too complicated
Anyway

It was so easy
To do one task one way
Every day;

To own the means
And to satisfy physical needs
One must own the control lines

How did legislating poverty oppress?

Victim of process
Had no access
Or no address.

For the paver of every new path
Needed a light to shine
In order to grow during the night.

You will be born alone and die alone.
Best to have a heart of stone
For Monopolistic Man

Says he is the only one who can
Unseal fate
To free you to be who you can be.

For Monopolistic Man
Owned Power and Might
While fake light shone during the night

THE STARE: Hidden Included

Easing Paralyzing Fright

Even though Fear was the tool
Of Monopolistic Man; a shell of a man;
Giving more might to a fool.

Love could change his ways
For Love was allowed to define you
Until the end of your days

Under this ever changing sky.

II

You were so classified
They lied as you cried
While the cause of your pain was denied

A nickname was given
To symbolize
Your place so social

The stare glared out their hate,
To justify their rule so cultural,
Love was delayed, and arrived too late.

Without love
It was so easy
To discriminate

For how could they know how to tolerate?

Victim of process
Had no access
Or no address.

They were so dehumanized
They criticized his tone
As they laughed

He was all alone.

The watchers were organized
Fallen angels from above
Easier for them to hate than to love

So polarized
In misunderstanding
Lost communication channels

Hate grew from different angles
Euphemisms were said
As a heart was stolen

THE STARE: Hidden Included

And resold
For gold
And treasure

Filling their lives with pleasure
A new future was in the air
The mass did not know how to prepare

In a polarized world with so little care
Polarization was never fair
And to fight for love made heroes of some

How did legislating poverty oppress?

Victim of process
Had no access
Or no address.

Though many would trade
Their water and air
For cold cash which just got devalued;

While others waited for the sun
To shine again
After the rain

The air smelled so sweet.
While the ones on their list
Were watched day after day

Made future persecutions more neat.

Dumped in a desert
Without food for mind nor heart
The vulture culture

Tore many apart;
Said to be no longer human
For they had lost their heart.

And Traded
Their water and air
For cold cash which just got devalued;

Victim of process
Had no access
Or no address.

And in the sky
There was a toxic cloud
Talking about it was not allowed

THE STARE: Hidden Included

Warm air rose into the cold
Violent gusts of wind
Moved the toxic cloud

Over our heads;
Monopolistic Man; a shell of a man;
Still takes what he can

Exterminated
Those he hated
While the tears dropped gently from the sky.

How did legislating poverty oppress?

Victim of process
Had no access
Or no address.

So demoralized;
Could not walk or talk nor cry,
The pain was so subjective

And some stood apart
And saved
Their heart.

And some were too
Willing to believe the lie
So they did not have to cry.

III

Monopolistic Man had his glossy magazine;
If you didn't look like a super model
He would treat you real mean.

Your pain was your chain;
They said Divine Love
Came from above;

You knew that real love
Could only come
From a pure heart;

So dehumanized
Was Monopolistic Man
His fat stomach got in the way

As he ran;

Toward a promise
That was already broken
And he too had pain which had awoken.

THE STARE: Hidden Included

The promise was misleading;
It promised love
Without any feeling;

And now Monopolistic man
Was close to ruin;
What was unfair could not be proven;

For the ruiner
Did not care what was at stake
And gave very few an even break.

Monopolistic Man could not help but stare;
There was so much suspicion in the air.
Monopolistic Man; a shell of a man;

Hoped that something was wrong

For he had far less than you;
While his jealousy grew
Into malice and false pride.

Monopolistic Man
Hoped for something to control
Then his stare fell upon you;

He traded
His water and air
For cold cash which just got devalued

Made him madder
As the green devil
Took over his head;

Monopolistic Man; a shell of a man;
Wished that you were dead.
He did everything he could to humiliate

He was a slave to Hate

Which paved his fate.
When his energy ran out
It was then too late.

How did legislating poverty oppress?

Victim of process
Had no access
Or no address.

THE END

HIDDEN

HIDDEN
I

Standing above
Without love
Subjectively

Selfishly
Hypocritically
Eyes refusing to see

The more they persecuted
The more they feared
The persecuted

During the denigration
No hope for negotiation
No concern for humanization

It is said there is a back door
For
Image I Nation

Hard to find
When one is blinded
By degradation

THE STARE: Hidden Included

A hurt sensation
For the last Generation
Without a title

The more they persecuted
The more they feared
The persecuted

Hold on for the Push
Stand tall for the Pull
Consume until full

By those hidden behind blank eyes so dull
As they push and shove
To get ahead in their culture without love

To speak out was never enough
Unreasonable, Unsustainable
Behind a wall, so much is unattainable

The more they persecuted
The more they feared
The persecuted

Their side of the street
Was behind a wall of concrete
Where they had never enough to eat

Where life moved to the speed of a crawl

Treated like bugs
Undeserving of hugs
Labelled as slugs

The more they persecuted
The more they feared
The persecuted

People crossed the street
Refused to integrate
Felt too much hate

Called the persecuted thugs
Fear was now mixed with hate
Lack of co-operation controlled fate

Successful denigration
Look away
Don't try negotiation

THE STARE: Hidden Included

Do as the label implies
Do not hear their painful cries
For now they have been ghettoized.

The more they persecuted
The more they feared
The persecuted

Behind the wall
So unethical
Still looking for the back door

May be just mythical
Truly unsustainable
Ghettoized

When they were young and able

II
Manipulation
Dehumanization
Forbidden and hidden

Distain
Complain
Detain

So denigrated
Trapped in a force of hatred
Nothing was negotiated.

The more they persecuted
The more they feared
The persecuted

For they are now all behind the wall.
Looking for a back door
So they can escape what has happened before

Wood-chipper diplomacy
No evidence based democracy
Seen by eyes closed in prayer

Eyes that would not see
As if the victims
Were not there

Paralyzed by bureaucracy;

THE STARE: Hidden Included

Totalitarian control
No longer able
To change their role

No longer believing
In the power
Of Soul

Push and shove
Culture without love
Believed cruelty was justified

The more they persecuted
The more they feared
The persecuted

Prayed for a greater might
Left the homeless
Destitute in middle of the night

Bulldozed whatever they could
To create their super-highway
Of push and shove

A world without love

The legacy
Of totalitarian control
No more time for a leisurely stroll

The more they persecuted
The more they feared
The persecuted

This was Wood-Chipper Diplomacy
Cutting down every tree
Which might be blocking a view or two

So denigrated
It was hard to not
Return the hatred

Just another trap
On the dead-end
Road to hell

Denigration
Force destroying one's value
Defamation

THE STARE: Hidden Included

So dictated
Made some sadistic
Others valued this power of hatred

The more they persecuted
The more they feared
The persecuted

So attached to the food chain politic

The more they persecuted
The more they feared
The persecuted

Could turn it all around
As technology helped the damaged
Take back their ground

Persecution so cruel
Mistreatment meant to drive away
Rivals and competition

Now the process
Could be turned around
The persecutors said

Feeding the persecuted was said to be wrong
For the persecuted would grow too strong
Could turn the process all around.

The cause for Malice was hidden
Entry into the wrong-way zone
Was forbidden

The more they persecuted
The more they feared
The persecuted

As the flood waters moved in
Black Bird from afar
Made her nest

In the hole in the wall.
And sang a song
As the promise of a new world

Moved along time
That never stood still
For that was the way of the Will.

THE END

Produced by S.E. McKenzie Productions
First Print Edition April 2015

Enquiries: 1(778)992-2453
Mailing Address:
S. E. McKenzie Productions
168 B 5th St.
Courtenay, BC
V9N 1J4

Email Address:
messidartha@aol.com

http://www.amazon.com/SarahMcKenzie/e/B00H9RWX48/ref=ntt
_dp_epwbk_0

www.ingramcontent.com/pod-product-compliance
Lightning Source LLC
Chambersburg PA
CBHW060547030426
42337CB00021B/4469